My Aunt's Book of Silent Actors

ANCESTORS
IN THE ATTIC

My Aunt's Book of
Silent Actors

MICHAEL HOLROYD

PIMPERNEL
PRESS LTD
www.pimpernelpress.com

Pimpernel Press Limited
www.pimpernelpress.com

ANCESTORS IN THE ATTIC
My Aunt's Book of Silent Actors
© Pimpernel Press Limited 2017
Text and illustrations © Michael Holroyd 2017

A catalogue record for this book is available from the British Library.

Designed by Anne Wilson
Typeset in Addington

ISBN 978-1-910258-84-2

Printed and bound in China
by C&C Offset Printing Company Limited

9 8 7 6 5 4 3 2 1

Frontispiece: My aunt, Yolande Phyllis Holroyd (1902–1998), in about 1923.

Contents

THE STORY
6

How a Lost Book Reached My Aunt
6

Enter the Actors
9

THE ACTORS
18

The Family
56

The Story

HOW A LOST BOOK REACHED MY AUNT

It had begun as a *Book of Ferns*, which my great-grandmother, Anne Eliza Holroyd, created in India during the early 1870s. But it was put aside after her tragic death in 1880, at the age of thirty.

My great-grandparents' two sons had been born in India, but their daughter, Norah Palmer, was born at the family's new home in Eastbourne early in 1877 and was not quite three years old when her mother died. While her two brothers were to be educated at boarding schools, Norah Palmer was brought up by a governess at home. In the autumn of 1896 her father passed on to her the *Book of Ferns*. Norah was by then aged nineteen. She wrote her name on the opening page of the book, underlining the date: 'Norah Palmer Holroyd. 18 Septr.1896'. She was a fragile young woman. 'My daughter is so poorly I regret I cannot ask anyone to the House,' her father wrote shortly before Christmas 1896 to Oscar Browning (an Old Etonian usually more interested in boys than girls). Early the following year Charles Holroyd had a stroke and was left partly paralysed. He was to die at their house in Eastbourne on 18 September 1898, a month short of his seventy-sixth birthday.

In his will he left everything his wife had owned (including her jewellery and ornaments) to his daughter. The residuary estate was left to the three children equally. Yet it is not quite equal. Norah Palmer's capital is to be retained by her trustees 'for as long as she shall remain unmarried and whether she shall be competent or incompetent to give legal discharge'. In the event of her marriage the income from this capital is to be 'for her separate use free from control and without power of alienation'. The money vested in her then passes to her children, but not before they are twenty-five. If she does not marry, or marries without having any children, then the capital sum (the income from which she has 'enjoyed' during her lifetime) is to be shared after her death by her two brothers, Patrick and Fraser. All this is carefully designed to protect her from men who might be tempted to marry her for money.

My grandparents, Fraser and Adeline Holroyd, with my father, Basil (sitting beside his mother), and his siblings Kenneth and Yolande, in about 1914.

In the last year of his life her father (whose estate was valued at over £18,000 – equivalent to more than £5 million pounds by 2016) made arrangements for his daughter to live at Beaufort House, which had become her home from home, at Ham in Surrey. The house belonged to a doctor who had been a surgeon-major in the Indian army. His daughter had married Eric Danvers Macnamara, a psychiatrist who practised there as well as in Harley Street in London. He specialized in mental and nervous diseases and wrote papers for medical journals about what was called 'functional insanity'. Norah Palmer was placed in the care of Eric Macnamara and his wife, Mary (of whom she became very fond). Norah's father wished them to care for her after his death.

It is impossible to know whether or not Norah Palmer suspected that her mother and one of her maternal aunts were subject to severe depression intensified by the birth of their children and that she may have inherited something of this 'mental disease'. Her father may have explained to her something of this danger, so that she would understand why she was being treated differently from her brothers in his will – as well as why she was in the care of a psychiatrist. I do not believe he would have wished her to think that she was being given a position inferior to that of her brothers simply on the grounds of being a woman.

My father remembered seeing his aunt Norah once, when he was very young. He had been told she was delicate, but thought her very kind to a small child. This may have been early in 1913, before Norah suddenly decided to travel abroad. Perhaps she needed to make a family visit to explain to her brothers why in the will she had recently made she was not leaving them anything. Since she was not married and had no children, her capital (£11,992. 6s.) would on her death be divided between these two brothers. For her to give them still more would be excessive. The main beneficiaries of her possessions were to be Mary Macnamara and Mary's husband, the psychiatrist. But, as a token of family affection, she was leaving some items to her brothers' children, her nephews and nieces. By this arrangement the *Book of Ferns* eventually came to my aunt: woman to woman.

Norah Palmer was to die on 22 October 1913 at Vernet-les-Bains in the south-west of France. No cause of death is given. It is as if she simply ceased living. She was thirty-six, six years older than her mother was when she died. There is no mention of her being pregnant. She had come through her life without passing on an ill-omened destiny. She may have decided to die there, though, beyond the frontiers of psychological treatment, she could have been searching for a miraculous cure in the magical waters of this spa town.

It was seventeen years since Norah had written her signature on the first page of her mother's *Book of Ferns* and made it her own. On her visit to her brother Fraser, my grandfather, she arranged for it to go to his daughter, my aunt Yolande, who was to be the third woman to own this book.

ENTER THE ACTORS

The album seems not to have reached my aunt until the end of the First World War. Between the approximate ages of sixteen and twenty she was to make her own very different contribution. The book had been on a long journey, travelling from India to England and covering almost fifty years, before Yolande contributed to it. What we see in this album is a different culture and technology, as well as a change in the social history of a family.

Leaving an empty page following a series of ferns, my aunt began to fill almost a hundred pages with pictures of actresses and actors, many of whom had left the theatre to become film stars in the new movies. She had no knowledge that these blank pages had been evidence of her aunt's devastating postnatal depression. Yolande filled these spaces with entertainers, displaying what amounts to a pictorial chapter of silent films in the early 1920s.

I turn the pages of the album. The first photo-portrait is of Mary Pickford. In a full-skirted satin dress with its lace-hemmed bodice and her shepherdess ringlets, she looks up provocatively through the years. She is followed on the next page by Charlie Chaplin smiling admiringly down at his co-star – a dog named Scraps – in a film called *A Dog's Life* (a title I later used for a novel).

Pickford and Chaplin were the two richest and most popular stars of silent films and their names still live with us. My aunt cut out and kept many pictures of them both. Mary Pickford appears as a sea siren with abandoned wind-and-water-swept hair, her bare feet cavorting over the sands (a perfect subject for what would later be called 'British Impressionism'); and then, as if in a pantomime, looking so tiny opposite the masculine bulk of her 'strong and tender lover', the hefty, long-forgotten American actor Thomas Meighan. Whether she is playing with a baby or sitting next to her pet dog (quite small but somehow larger than she is) while they wait for her husband to return home, these publicity photographs show her as the embodiment of innocence and youthfulness. Charlie Chaplin is oddly at ease in what look like tall riding boots, jodhpurs and a tweed jacket — something between a jockey and a golf player. More characteristic is a picture of him in 1921 grasping the hand of Jackie Coogan in *The Kid*. This was a celebrated film on the controversial subject of illegitimacy which he wrote and directed and in which he starred. My aunt added a memorable picture of the young Jackie Coogan alone, crouched down smoking a cigarette, alert for trouble, the perfect image of an artful dodger.

In 1919 Pickford and Chaplin, together with the pioneering director D.W. Griffith and the 'King of Hollywood', Douglas Fairbanks, had founded the motion picture company United Artists. My aunt scissored out a couple of Fairbanks's images, one of them as a swashbuckling cowboy politely introducing us to his horse, the second as the athletic d'Artagnan in *The Three Musketeers*. This came out in 1921, the year after he married Mary Pickford.

Another actress whose portraits my aunt particularly liked was 'The First Lady of the American Cinema', Lillian Gish, a childhood friend of Mary Pickford. On some of the pages of the album it would be difficult to recognize her without the identifying captions. On one page she wears a vast hat trimmed with worrying feathers; on another she is wrapped in furs and crowned with an array of ripe fruit; she appears again as a bewilderingly slender figure with huge batwings and

The house in Maidenhead where Yolande collected the pictures.

a clinging skirt; and finally, with her hair piled up high on the page as part of a delicate Japanese composition, she raises her fan and tilts her head engagingly towards us. Such a variety of images suggests her wide range as an actress. She is essentially a romantic star, as opposed to her sister Dorothy Gish, who was known as a comedian and sometimes looks rather cross. They acted together in several films. but Lillian's fame outlasted Dorothy's. The fashions of beauty turn and turn again – and still go on. Contemporary jokes have their moments: then silently fade away forever. Even now, when there is no more silence, what we see probably lasts longer than what we hear. (But at the end, when we are unconscious, we can hear but not see who is beside the bed: so be careful what you say.)

The careers of many of these actors began to disappear after the talkies arrive. But Bebe Daniels, who is also on my aunt's pages (unfortunately got up at as a ridiculous Santa Claus climbing on to a pedestal), was to be an exception. With her husband, Ben Lyon, she left Hollywood in the mid-1930s and came to London, where they worked for the British Broadcasting Corporation. I remember enjoying their sitcom *Life with the Lyons* on the radio in my early teens and seeing them later when the programmes were transferred to television.

Except to cinema scholars of this period, the household names of many much-loved performers have now faded. The immortality of fame is brief – a sobering lesson for celebrities yesterday and tomorrow. The women in my aunt's pictures draw attention with their provokingly bare shoulders, their skirts like lampshades and tastefully plunging necklines; also with the flowers that rest copiously in their laps and on the hats they hold like shields protecting their bodies. Looking wistful and somewhat accusatory, these women resemble children behaving as adults. They toy with sexual symbols such as the offering of a key, and strike Grecian poses, their gigantic sleeves emphasizing their slender bodies. Some of the beach beauties wear knickers that peep out from their skirts (indicating they were very slow swimmers). Occasionally they appear to be wearing nothing more than an innocent towel.

But the men are heavily covered with many layers of clothing: huge highwaymens' overcoats, solid three-piece suits with tightly buttoned-up waistcoats, ties bisecting their shirts and a suggestion of vests. They are well-groomed gentlemen with shining patent shoes. The gentleman-seducers wear meaningful smiles and carry bottles of champagne; the villainous gentlemen arrive with capes covering their shoulders. The most impressive of all these gentleman callers is identified by the word 'Lucifer!' Some of these desperate men hold on to things – watches, pipes, cigarettes and even the edge of the page, as if they might suddenly fall off it into hideous oblivion. They had not spoken in their films and on my aunt's pages they cannot move. They strive, it seems, to hold my attention and be seen. Then I turn the pages and one by one they are gone.

Then on one of these pages I see someone whose name I know very well. Owen Nares was a matinee idol of the 1920s and the star of several silent melodramas and romances including *The Private Life of Don Juan* and *The Sorrows of Satan.* I never saw him in these films but I heard about him from his son David Nares, an advertising executive for Martini cocktails. He was one of several people whom my mother married and they lived during the late 1950s in an apartment below a famous publisher, George Weidenfeld, overlooking the Thames in Chelsea. In the publicity photograph of Owen Nares, his wavy hair has been cut short and is strictly under control. His tie, with its myriad white dots like stars in the sky, is impeccably knotted like some mysterious dark matter. He looks younger than his son and is the very model of a model English gentleman. I give him a curt salute learnt from my National Service days in the army, then turn the page and am taken back by something unexpected.

The next five pages are suddenly full of Indian ferns, as if my great-grandmother had come alive again. They are separated from the previous ferns by thirty-five pages of my aunt's quiet film stars. Had she known the story of these ferns and the significance of the empty pages, pages of nothing, pages of despair, she might have hesitated. The intermittent scatterings of ferns and groups of actors pursue one another through the middle of the album, as if pessimism and optimism were in conversation, outdoors and indoors, youth and maturity coming and going like time itself. But the number of actors overwhelms the few ferns. After a further fifteen comedians there is a single page with an arrangement of three ferns in a semi-oval outline. Then another ten pages appear with actresses dancing on a beach, playing a pianola, travelling on a sleigh, as if to cheer us up, make us forget. For the reader this is a roller-coaster journey. It illustrates the difficulty of interpreting the past. The empty white pages I see as pages of darkness and death; the pages of cinema actors as an invitation to romance and laughter.

The other parts of the album give glimpses of my aunt's character in her late teens. By the age of twenty-one she has stopped pasting in these silent women and men who had been her favourite film stars. She continues for a time carefully cutting them out of magazines but no longer pastes them into the waiting pages. They are crowded loosely at the end of the album like actors eternally waiting in the wings. I begin to feel some sympathy for them being unable to reach a page – they seem to struggle with one another as if for a cinema audience. I must give them some lines.

Almost all of them are American actresses and actors – my aunt appearing to be more interested in the women than the men. Many of them were to enjoy successful careers and end up on the celebrated Hollywood Walk of Fame. But in the early 1920s, when my aunt was still scissoring them from the newspaper world, these women and men were making their careers in what was called the 'entertainment industry'. Some had begun astonishingly young: Blanche Sweet started at the age of four; Clara Kimball when she was three. An exception to those who had shot to stardom and faded with the advent of talkies was Betty Compson, a busy actress who had studied the violin and liked singing silently, which she continued to do in the talkies when her actual voice was dubbed by a woman who actually could sing but was less attractive.

My aunt did not know the careers of these young people any more than she knew her own future life. She did not need to know more. These actors were her own fictional characters and would soon belong to her past. But now they have had the misfortune of falling into the hands of a biographer.

I have found out more about her actresses, many of whom married twice or three times (two of them married the same man twice). Clara Cronk changed her name to Claire Windsor – which must have helped her succeed in winning parts as 'upscale society girls'. She also had romances with several male co-stars. Agnes Ayres played the Latin lover of Rudolph Valentino in *The Sheikh* and then *Son of the Sheikh*, after which she was too hefty to play anyone. Harriet Hammond was a splendidly athletic bathing beauty who took on powerful comic parts in *Gee Whiz!* and *By Golly!* before joining the Ziegfeld Follies on Broadway. To the irritation of several other actresses, Carol Dempster took on major roles in films directed by D.W. Griffith, starting with *Intolerance*, and then became his mistress until retiring in comfort with a bank manager.

But some stories my aunt must have picked up, because she also stuck in a few sentences from the magazines she had read. So she knew that Dorothy Dalton, on discovering that she could not play mature women, specialized as vamps and became famous for breaking the hearts of cameramen. 'I guess I must have been born that way,' she explained.

There is only one British actor among the men without pages in my aunt's book. He is Percy Marmont, best remembered for playing the title role of Conrad's Lord Jim in 1915. Of the Americans, Buck Jones was famous for not being Buck Jones the American football player or the other Buck Jones the hockey enthusiast. My aunt's Buck Jones was a Western movie man. In her photograph of him he sits in deep thought, unaware of the strange figure of Patsey de Forest, who starred in *Help! Help! Help!* He is unmoved while she looks lovingly down on him from the top of what appears to be an agonizingly uncomfortable wall. Matt Moore in one of his 221 films is seen with his loyal pipe and easy smile, his mind apparently elsewhere. Wallace Reid is a pleasantly attractive man who sits with his excellent dog under one arm and a rifle under his other. He is gazing into a happy future which, this biographer knows, will never arrive.

My aunt, having shoved these characters in the back of her book, is no longer a mere spectator of stories: she is going to parties now, meeting people, travelling abroad, entering an exciting and romantic world that had previously entranced her in the cinemas. Early photographs show her as having been very attractive. She looked forward to the life to come. There are several love letters she kept to the end of her life. She must surely marry soon. But no story from the silent films could have prepared her for what was to happen. On the screen they show us happy days only.

At the end of the Second World War, when I was nine or ten, my aunt began taking me to the two cinemas in Maidenhead, the Plaza and the Rialto. Though neither of us knew it, we both needed to enter worlds of fiction and fantasy. She liked musicals, I preferred cartoons and thrillers. I would wait for these vicarious adventures with intense excitement. In my early years, films released me into other lives as, I believe, they had once taken my aunt.

I was very proud of her. She had taken a job as a telephone operator in the post office during the war. Somehow I got the impression that her work was secret — crucial to winning our battles. This was probably because I confused this night-time job with her intermittent day job driving library books to German prisoner of war camps.

Later on we would sometimes play gentle games of tennis together, making sure that no one lost. In other ways she seemed rather strange. Even in the pouring rain she preferred to have her breakfast in the garden with the birds rather than with the family. Much of her day was given up to walking many miles with her Labrador, which came back exhausted. In the evening she retired

Me, around the time I started going to the cinema in Maidenhead with
Aunt Yolande.

into her bedroom. I could tell from the way she closed her door on us that something had gone wrong, but only came to understand it many years later.

She loved her father but found it difficult to be in the same room as her mother. A love affair which her father had while Yolande was in her mid-twenties was to complicate her life. In the 1920s, while he was living elsewhere, he sent her a special payment 'for your wedding clothes'. But when he returned some three or four years later his daughter was still unmarried. The scandal of her father's adultery, as well as his desperate financial predicament, had thrown a shadow over the marriage. The chief obstacle was her mother, who insisted that Yolande's duty was to remain by her side during the crisis, threatening suicide if she left. Gradually Yolande was to become imprisoned in the house. She stayed on to keep an eye on her father and make his life endurable. During the 1930s there was, however, a man she loved. Their understanding was that they would marry when things got better: this year, next year, sometime soon . . . During the war he joined the army and was posted to Italy, eventually coming back with one of the enemy, a young Italian girl, whom he had married. Although I saw my aunt every day, I never heard anyone speak of this. The bedroom became her world and her silence reached us all.

Later I discovered that this man she loved was a fantasist who lived several parallel lives, changing his name, inventing his parents, and secretly marrying several times – the last time on his deathbed in hospital. Though apparently poor, he owned, at one time or another, a racing car, a yacht and a biplane. Latterly he lived in a block of London flats favoured by spies and secret agents. None of this my aunt ever knew.

Following a stroke, my aunt was to leave Maidenhead, take to a wheelchair and become silent, though often smiling, sometimes even appearing to laugh. She seemed released from tragedy into contentment, having apparently forgotten her dream days and the distress that followed them. She died in her mid-nineties. It was only when revisiting Maidenhead after her death that I was handed this hidden book carrying her early film stars which had been left in the attic.

The history of this album goes back now almost a hundred and fifty years. First my great-grandmother Anne Eliza had filled many pages with ferns. Then her daughter, Norah Palmer, signed into it. And finally my aunt populated it with the silent movie stars who had enriched her teenage years. Now the album has come to me. And I have endeavoured to hand its contents to readers.

A watercolour portrait of Aunt Yolande, at about the age of twenty.

The Actors

Mary Pickford (8 April 1892–29 May 1979). Mary Pickford and Charlie Chaplin were the two richest and most popular stars of silent films. My aunt cut out and kept many pictures of them both.

MARY PICKFORD

19

The hefty, long-forgotten American actor Thomas Meighan (9 April 1879–8 July 1936) and Mary Pickford, in *M'liss* (1918), in which Thomas Meighan played Charles Gray and Mary Pickford Melissa 'M'liss' Smith.

"Just as high as his Heart"

THOMAS MEIGHAN, "a strong, tender lover," with MARY PICKFORD in "M'liss."

CHARLIE CHAPLIN

Oddly at ease in tall riding boots, jodhpurs and a tweed jacket, something between a jockey and a golf player, Charlie Chaplin (16 April 1889–25 December 1977). In 1919, Pickford and Chaplin, together with the pioneering director D. W. Griffith and the 'King of Hollywood', Douglas Fairbanks, founded the motion picture company United Artists.

Charlie Chaplin and Jackie Coogan (26 October 1914–1 March 1984) in *The Kid* (1921), written, produced and directed by Chaplin. Coogan played Chaplin's adopted son and sidekick.

Jackie Coogan in *The Kid* – alert for trouble . . . the perfect image of an artful dodger.

JACKIE COOGAN—"THE KID"

27

'The King of Hollywood', Douglas Fairbanks (23 May 1883–12 December 1939), in *The Three Musketeers* (1921). Fairbanks had married Mary Pickford in 1920.

DOUGLAS FAIRBANKS as D'ARTAGNAN

'The First Lady of American Cinema', Lillian Gish (14 October 1893–27 February 1993), and her sister Dorothy Gish (11 March 1898–4 June 1968). Lillian Gish was a childhood friend of Mary Pickford. She was essentially a romantic star, while Dorothy Gish was known as a comedian (and sometimes looks rather cross). The sisters acted together in several films, but Lillian's fame has long outlived Dorothy's.

SALOME.

The Russian-born actress Alla Nazimova (*c.* 1881–1945) in *Salome* (1923), based on the Oscar Wilde play. Although little remembered today, Alla Nazimova was a major star of Broadway in the early twentieth century.

Claire Windsor (14 April 1892–24 October 1972) was born Clara Viola Cronk and nicknamed 'Ola'. She changed her name to Claire Windsor, which must have been a help in winning parts as princesses and wealthy socialites – 'upscale society girls'.

CLAIRE WINDSOR

Agnes Ayres (4 April 1898–25 December 1940), seen here in *Forbidden Fruit* (1921). She is best known for playing the Latin lover of Rudolph Valentino in *The Sheikh* (1921) and *Son of the Sheikh* (1926), after which she was too hefty to play anyone.

AGNES AYRES
Now starring in "Forbidden Fruit"
Paramount

Harriet Hammond (20 October 1899–23 September 1991), a splendidly athletic bathing beauty (she was one of Mack Sennett's *Bathing Beauties*) who took on powerful comic parts in *Gee Whiz!* and *By Golly!* before joining the Ziegfeld Follies on Broadway.

'Mack Sennett, the Flo. Ziegfeld of the screen, has no prize beauty of whom he is more proud than the blonde Harriet Hammond. Miss Hammond is an example of such unusual pulchritude, that the chains she wears across her shoulder are entirely unnecessary for the enslavement of her beholders.'

HARRIETT HAMMOND

Mack Sennett, the Flo Ziegfeld of the screen, has no priz beauty of whom he is more proud than the blonde Harriett Hammond. Miss Hammond is an example of such unusual pulchritude, that the chains she wears across her shoulder are entirely unnecessary for the enslavement of her beholders.

Dorothy Dalton (22 September 1893–13 April 1972). Dorothy specialized in playing vamps, and became famous for breaking the hearts of cameramen. 'I guess I must have been born that way,' she explained.

DOROTHY DALTON

IRENE CASTLE TREMAINE

Irene Castle (17 April 1893–25 January 1963) was a 'lithesome and facetious' dancer who achieved huge fame with her husband and dance partner English-born Vernon Castle (2 May 1887–15 February 1918). Vernon was killed in a plane crash in the First World War. Irene later married Robert E. Tremaine.

Owen Nares (11 August 1888–30 July 1943) was a matinee idol of the 1920s and the star of several melodramas and romances, including *The Private Life of Don Juan* and *The Sorrows of Satan*. His son, David Nares — an advertising executive for Martini cocktails — was one of several people whom my mother married.

Buck Jones (12 December 1891–30 November 1942), a Western movie man, but more famous for being neither Buck Jones the American football star nor Buck Jones the hockey player. In this photograph, from 1920, Buck sits deep in thought, unmoved as Patsey de Forest (1 May 1888–1966) looks lovingly down on him from what appears to be an agonizingly uncomfortable wall.

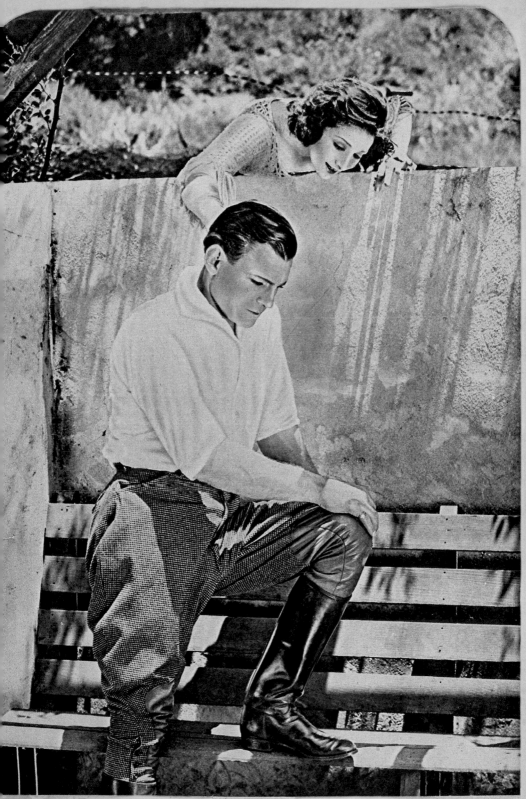

PEACE TERMS.

Matt Moore (8 January 1888–21 January 1960), with his loyal pipe and easy smile. Born in Ireland, he arrived in the US with his siblings via Ellis Island in 1898. He made 221 films. His brother Owen was briefly married to Mary Pickford.

MATT MOORE

WALLACE REID

Wallace Reid (15 April 1891–18 January 1923). A pleasantly attractive man who sits with his excellent dog under one arm and rifle in the other. He is gazing into a happy future which, this biographer knows, will never arrive. (He became addicted to morphine following an injury in a train crash, and died in a sanatorium at the age of thirty-one.)

A sad parting.

The Parting

Nina Sands &

WHO WILL SPEAK FIRST?

A lovers' quarrel between Spanish-born American actor Antonio Moreno (26 September 1887–15 February 1957) and Jean Calhoun (1 April 1891–25 August 1958) in *Three Sevens* (1921).

A Lovers' Quarrel between ANTONIO MORENO and JEAN CALHOUN—in " Three Sevens."

Charles Chaplin Holroyd = Virginie Mottet de la Fontaine

Thomas Smith = Delia

Mary Anne Rochfort
m. Robert Humphrey Sears — 4 sons
d. 11 February 1880, by suicide in Taunton

Janet Smith
m. John Stewart Paul
daughter 1, d. at 1 month,
daughter 2, Helena, 2 sons

Charles Holroyd = (2) 26 August 1872 Anne Eliza Smith
b. 1822 Hyderabad   b. 2 August 1849
d. 1898   d. 7 January 1880, by suicide in Glasgow

Mary Florence, widow of Colonel Hannay (1)
(2 sons by Colonel Hannay)
d. 1863 in India of apoplexy in childbirth

Edward Fraser Rochfort = 1899 Adeline Corbet
b. 1875 Calcutta   b. 1876
d. 1961   d. 1969

Norah Palmer
b. 30 January 1877 Eastbourne
d. 22 October 1913 in France

Charles Patrick
b. 1874 Calcutta
d. 1932

Ulla Knutsson-Hall = Basil Holroyd
b. 1916   b 1907
d. 1986   m. (1) 1934–47
                       m. (2) 1948–54
                       m. (3) 1958–67
                       d. 1988

Kenneth de Courcy
b. 1903
m. 1947
d. 1969

Dennis Sowley
b. 1900
d. 1900

Yolande Phyllis
b. 1902
d. 1998

Michael Holroyd
b. 1935

THE FAMILY